▲ *Wörlitz Castle* [**1**] *from the water*

As a result of his journeys through England, Italy, Germany, Holland, France, and Switzerland, Prince Franz encountered many ideas which stimulated his wish to transform his country. Together with his friend and advisor, Friedrich Wilhelm von Erdmannsdorff (1736–1800) and other true believers, he studied ancient architecture under the personal guidance of Winckelmann. Those responsible for the horticultural transformation of the landscape in Wörlitz and the surrounding area included, most notably, the gardener Johann Leopold Ludwig Schoch, Sr. (1728–1793) and his son Johann George (1758–1827), as well as Johann Christian Neumark, Johann Friedrich Eyserbeck and August Leopold Wöpke.

The layout of the Wörlitz garden grounds began in 1764 in the area surrounding a baroque castle and garden ensemble. There, at the

The numbers **1** to **58** refer to the map on page 30/31

banks of the Wörlitz Lake, a small landscaped park was developed with an English Pavilion and a swan pond. Soon after, other areas in the castle park and the surrounding countryside were reconfigured. The old castle was removed and the adjoining areas of the city were completely changed. Work on the northern park had significantly progressed when, in the years 1770 and 1771, floods destroyed the construction that had been completed in the northern low lying areas. These setbacks offered the opportunity to start again, with the benefit of knowledge gained from prior experience. Thus, the later garden areas have a different character from the early ones. While the castle park and Neumark garden are divided into small, regularly-shaped sections with less expressive design features, Schoch garden offers a series of spatially arranged, differentiated garden vistas, which open up as one proceeds on the guided path.

In the last decade of the eighteenth century, the gardener Johann George Schoch expanded the park and new garden grounds in the east. At the lake Große Walloch (Great Dike Hole) and around Rock ("Stone") Island, large bodies of water and agricultural fields were encircled by landscaped plants. These features received their creative highpoint with the addition of architectural characteristics in a style evoking "traveling impressions."

Wörlitz Gardens, Buildings, and Other Architectural Features

The four-armed Wörlitz Lake, a backwater of the Elbe River, is surrounded by a park area, which is divided into five discrete gardens. Two other lakes, the Große Walloch (Large Walloch) and the Kleine Walloch (Small Walloch), were created by water that had eroded the Elbe River's protective dyke. The lakes are linked by canals, which divide the terrain into individual plots. In each garden section, the architecture, bridges, and sculptures continuously form picturesque focal points which correlate with each other through connecting lines of sight. At these places of contemplation, the visitor is stimulated to engage in aesthetic appreciation as well as in reflection.

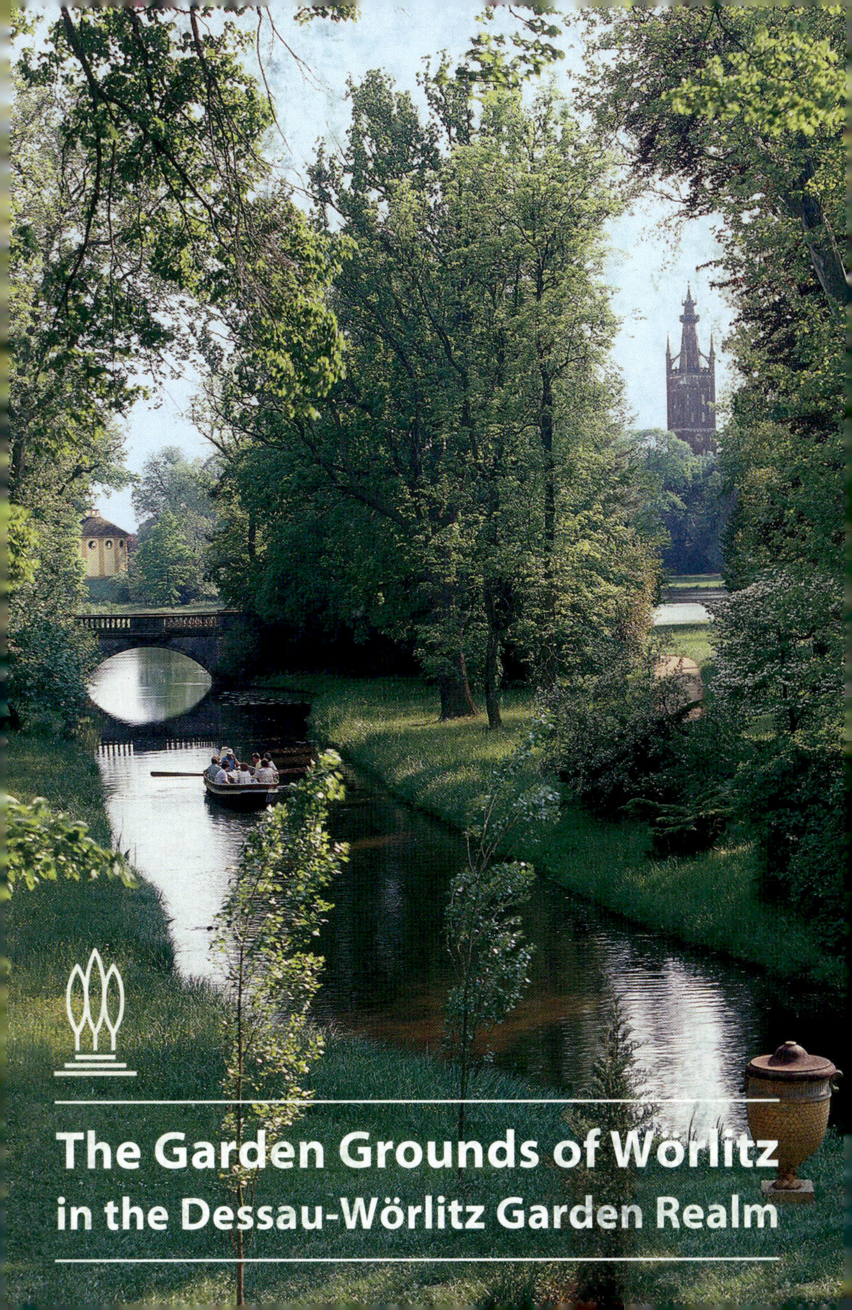

The Garden Grounds of Wörlitz

in the Dessau-Wörlitz Garden Realm

The Garden Grounds of Wörlitz

By Ludwig Trauzettel

Developed in the second half of the eighteenth century as the earliest landscaped garden in Central Europe, the garden grounds of Wörlitz are the heart of the Dessau-Wörlitz garden realm. When Prince Leopold Friedrich Franz (1740–1817) became regent in Anhalt-Dessau in 1758, he introduced multifaceted reforms, with youthful energy and daring, to advance his country's economy, wealth, and education. His embrace of new architectural and landscape garden-design principles reflected his enlightened-humanistic sensibility. In a way, the garden grounds of Wörlitz were an antithesis to the stringent and artificial Baroque style that was then customary. At Wörlitz, in accordance with Johann Joachim Winckelmann and Jean-Jacques Rousseau, the ideas of naturalness, simplicity and freedom were supposed to prevail. In beautifying the land, the goal was to create within the humble land of Anhalt-Dessau, a new holistic landscape aesthetic aligned with the classical ideal of fusing the beautiful and the useful. Arable land, fruit tree-lined roads, and forest edges were included in the artistic arrangement. The agricultural, mythological, architectural and art-historical content of educational programs was supposed to be communicated in an exemplary way through garden and landscape design. One aspect of this educational program is exemplified by the nineteen different bridges found on the Wörlitz grounds. They were built as demonstrations to the visitor of the development of the art of bridge construction with all its technical possibilities, from the simple tree trunk that spanned the shallows of river or stream to the most modern cast iron bridge. The exemplary English agriculture within the garden grounds was equally innovative and edifying, as were the Prince's efforts in the field of pomology (fruit cultivation) and the new architectural structures built in the neo-classical and gothic revival styles. The Wörlitz garden grounds, including the castle, were open to the public.

Front cover: *Canal with church* [**8**] and *synagogue* [**12**]

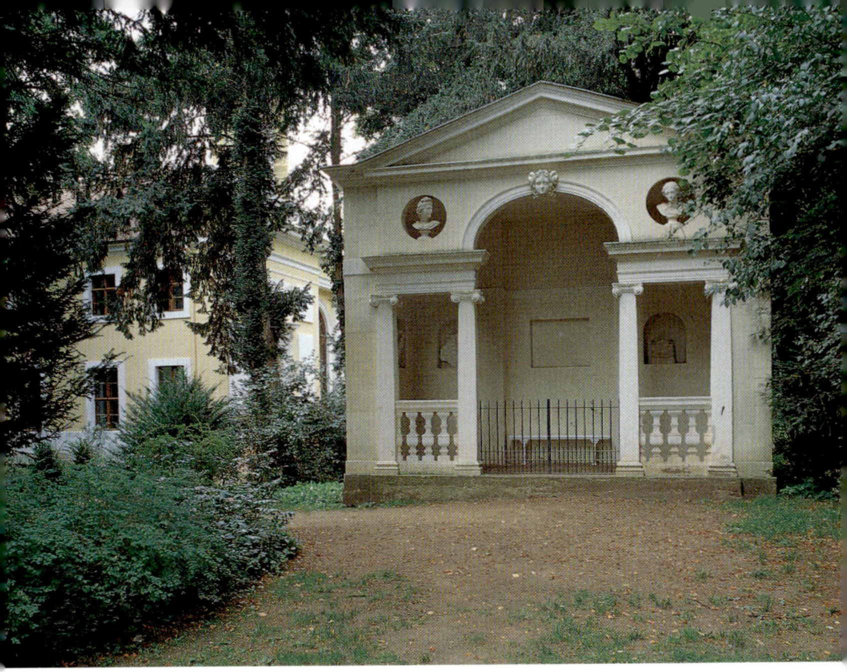

▲ *The English Pavilion* [2]

The Castle Garden

The layout of the Wörlitz Garden grounds began in 1764 with the castle, located south of Wörlitz Lake. Small, independent parts of the garden, such as the Garden at the Swan Pond, the Garden of the Princess, and the churchyard, are grouped around the castle meadow with the English country mansion (castle) and its farm buildings. In accordance with the design principles that came into use after 1765, the lime trees in the area were left uncut and allowed to grow freely. They transition into a natural landscape.

Work on the **Garden at the Swan Pond** began in 1764 and the still evolving design is reflected in the initial stage. A drawbridge, reconstructed in 2001, leads over the water where the pond enters into the lake. Its creative highpoint is the **English Pavilion** [2]. Built by

Erdmannsdorff in 1764/65, it is the earliest neo-classical building in Wörlitz. The plastered brick building was constructed as a garden abode with a view on to the Nymphaeum (1767/68), which was modelled after a no longer existing example in Stourhead (South England). It is outfitted with copies of antique marble sculptures. The architecture of the arch, column, and beams reflects a typical Palladio-motif and thereby evokes ancient architecture.

The **castle** [1], constructed by Erdmannsdorff between 1769 and 1773, is considered the founding structure of German neo-classicism. A columned hall with triangular pediment crowns is located to the side of the castle entrance. Also referred to as the "country mansion," the structure offers a three levelled Palladian architecture. The sculptures positioned in alcoves to the sides of the entry – Ceres, goddess of agriculture, and Fortuna, goddess of fortune and success – extend an invitation to the castle's museum (original interior design).

The **kitchen building** [3], located next to the castle and connected with the castle through an underground path, together with the summer hall, is a multi-purpose structure with a u-shaped ground plan. It originally housed the serving chambers. The summer hall, the neo-classical façade of which faces the castle, was used as a garden dining hall during the summer and as a greenhouse during the winter. It is decorated with statues of Apollo and a satyr by Gottfried Knöffler (1715–1779). The back of the building facing the church yard exhibits a provisional neo-Gothic design. Today, the kitchen building, erected by Ermannsdorff in 1770/72, houses the restaurant, the Garden Realm store, and the visitor centre. A fountain stands in front of the neo-classical façade of the summer hall. Made of sandstone and erected in 1774 as an **antique ara** (altar), the fountain was modelled after Winckelmann's Luna altar from his "Monumenti antici inedici." Within the neo-Gothic ensemble of the **church yard** stands the 4.50 meter high **sandstone fountain**, built in 1787 in a matching style. In 1785, the **sandstone urn** with a pine crest was placed across from the catering entrance of the kitchen building.

The **Dietrich Urn** [5] found at the entry of the **Garden of the Princess** [4] commemorates the uncle and guardian of the Prince, Dietrich

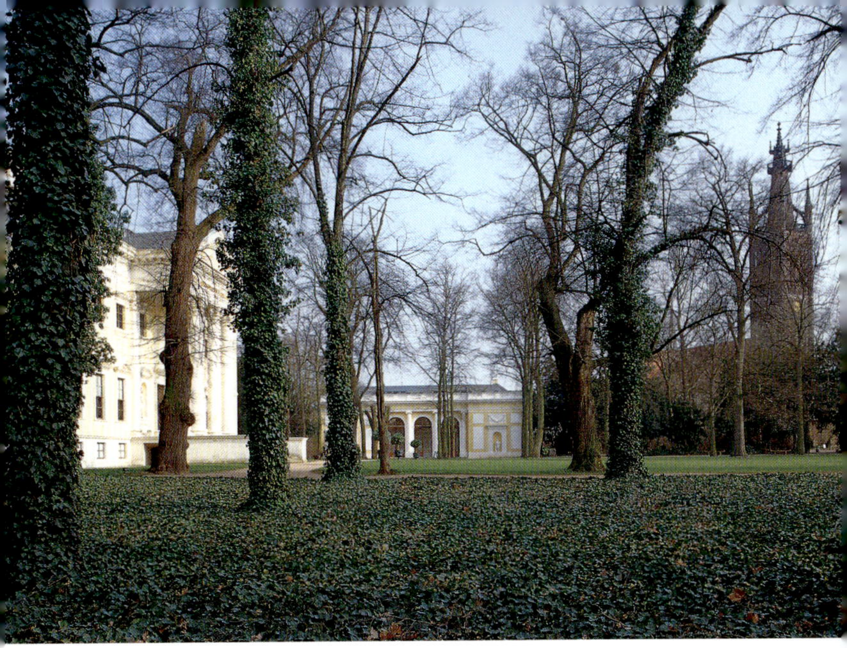

▲ *Castle* [**1**], *kitchen building* [**3**], *and church* [**8**] *viewed from the linden tree axis*

von Anhalt-Dessau (1702–1769), whose living quarters had once stood at this location and had been removed – as had elements of the city – during the expansion of the garden. The memorial, which, at its base, is decorated with four bas-reliefs, was created in 1775 by the sculptor Johann Christian Ehrlich and modelled on a drawing by Erdmannsdorff. In 1771, the adjoining Garden of the Princess was designed as a flower garden at the western lakeside of the castle garden. The house of the gondolier, the pheasantry, and the greenhouse were originally located here. After the demolition of the house of the gondolier, a tea pergola was erected around 1830. In 1934, under the guidance of Hallervorden (1872–1968), the director of the garden, efforts were made to modify and simplify the whole complex which had fallen into disrepair. The sandstone **ara** (altar), modelled on antique

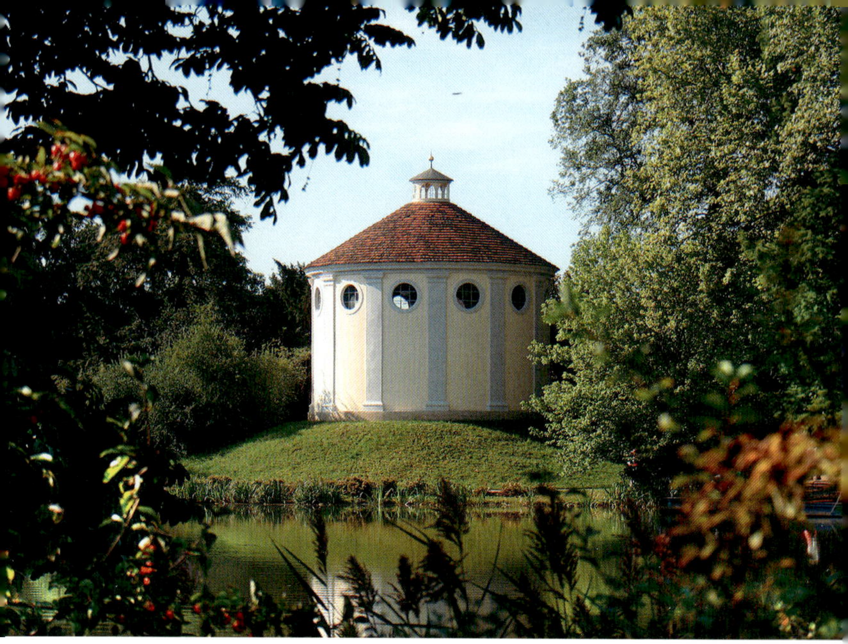

▲ *Synagogue* [**12**]

precursors, is dated from around 1770 and served as a fountain for those garden areas. The statue of the **nymph with a shell** [6] surrounded by sandstone vases and Lombardy poplars is located at the lake below the summer dining hall. It is a manufactured copy from 1771 of an antique sculpture of a girl playing knucklebone at the Villa Borghese in Rome. Further north of the shore next to the former boat dock, as well as along the path to the castle, there are (respectively) two female **sandstone herms**, dating from around 1765, the beginning phase of the castle garden's design.

The **churchyard**, which is east of the kitchen building and between the stables, the residence of the Princess, and the Probstei (Canonry), is an independent garden space, which once belonged to a Romanesque church, dating from 1200. Mortal remains found during the transformation of this area were buried under a **sarcophagus** [7]. Following Erdmannsdorff's instructions, the sandstone copy of the Roman Nero-sarcophagus was placed here in 1785/87. It is decorated with inscriptions from Klopstock texts and with representations of classical geniuses. Between 1804 and 1809, Prince Franz had his building director Georg Christoph Hesekiel reconstruct **St. Petri Church** [**8**] with its 66 meter (217 feet) high tower in a neo-Gothic style inspired by English and Flemish models. The eastern border of the churchyard is the **residence of the Princess** (Grey House) [**9**], the private abode of Princess Luise Henriette von Anhalt-Dessau (1750–1811). Inspired by Sheffield Place (southern England), it was erected in 1789/90 in a neo-Gothic style at the location of the former Probstei and expanded in 1850. The southern addition of the gallery (1804/05) was outfitted with a collection of literary and artistic treasures belonging to the Princess. Her small private garden was located behind the Grey House. The **Probstei** (Canonry) [**10**] south of the gallery, a neo-Gothic two-story brick building with a stepped gable, probably erected according to Erdmannsdorff's design in 1796, is nowadays the Protestant rectory of the city of Wörlitz. Together with the **Marstall** (castle stables) [**11**] and the neo-Gothic horse stable, the building represents the access point to the church from the city.

The **synagogue** [**12**] at the eastern edge of the castle garden was created as a central building by Erdmannsdorff. It was modelled after the Temple of Portunus on the river Tiber near Rome. The ritual bath is accessible from the street and is located below the prayer room. With its strictly functional organization of rooms, the architecture of the synagogue, Erdmannsdorff's only sacred building, answers to the needs of Jewish religious rituals and is a unique example of its kind in Europe. As a result of "Reichskristallnacht" ("Night of Broken Glass") in November 1938, the original interior design was completely destroyed. It was because of the decisive intervention of the garden custodian of the time, Hans Hallervorden, that the building itself was preserved.

"Eichenkranz" Inn ("Oak Wreath") [**13**], at the western edge of the castle garden, was built in 1785/87 by Erdmannsdorff for visitors to Wörlitz. The structure, which arches over the street, exhibits a half-timbered façade on the side of the city and a Gothicized gate-inspired fabrication on the garden side. **Friederike Bridge** [**14**] built in 1788 according to a design by Erdmannsdorff and expanded in 1940, is named after Princess Friederike from Prussia. It leads from the castle garden over one of the three outflows of Wörlitz Lake into the countryside.

Neumark Garden

Named after the gardener Johann Christan Neumark (1741–1811), the garden originally served as the princely agricultural garden. Because of its higher elevation, it – like the castle garden – was not destroyed during the flooding of 1770 and 1771. That is why the simple stylistic language of the earliest construction phase is still recognizable here. To the west and east, the garden area is surrounded by two branches of the Wörlitz Lake. To the south, a canal created around 1780 and running between the two lake branches screens the garden from the Wörlitz village common.

The garden can be reached either by ferry or by crossing the **Eisenhart Bridge** [**15**]. The bridge's arch spanning the canal with a rustic covering of bog iron ore, carries two pavilions erected by Erdmannsdorff between 1781 and 1784. The **South-Sea Pavilion**, a brick building with a pilaster arrangement and alcoves with round arches exhibits ethnographic items from the South-Sea. Prince Franz had acquired these objects from the humanist and world traveller Georg Forster (1754–1794). Until 1818, the **Library Pavilion**, covered on two façades with bog iron ore, housed a garden library, which Prince Franz opened to his guests and visitors. In the alcoves of the foyer, now housing a Wedgwood Shop, one will find cast replicas of a Bacchus, a Bacchante, and a faun. The **blind arch wall** crowned with a pergola for espalier fruit at the canal originally concealed the utility and residential quarters of the garden personnel. In the final alcove of the pergola sits a plaster reproduction of the antique statue of a praying boy. To the side is a **labyrinth** [**16**] dating from 1783/84. Not intended as a maze for courtly recreation, it was meant rather to be understood as an allegory of life (see August Rode, 1798, *Allegory of the Life of Prince Franz*). The meandering paths in this section of the garden

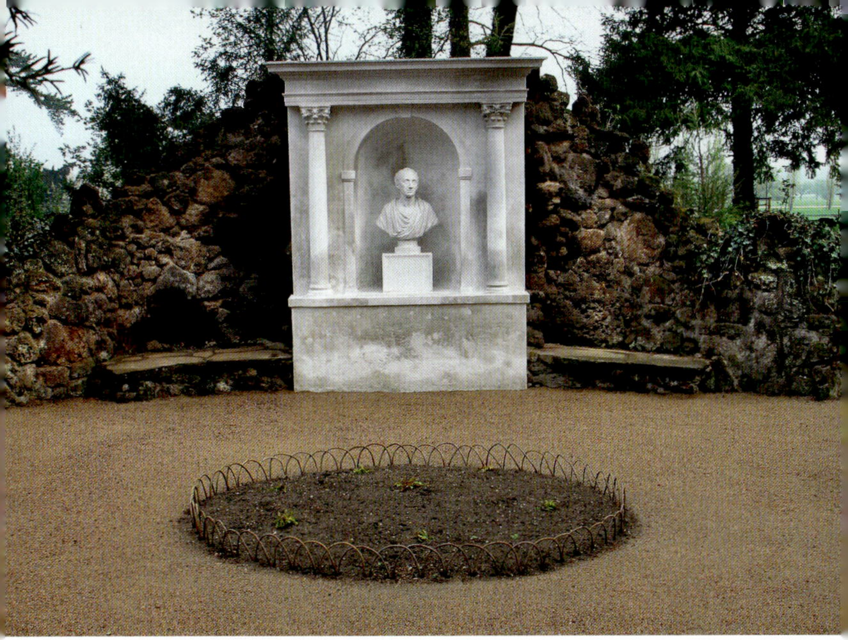

▲ *"Teachers influence on life" – allegorical section in the labyrinth* [**16**]

represent themselves as life journeys, influenced by companions, teachers and fellow human beings. At times, these paths can have a disorienting effect. Statues and inscribed tablets guide the thoughts of those who wander here. The busts of Lavater and Gellert are positioned at a clearing. Located in the grotto, Venus Lamia with the goose stands as a symbol of seduction and delusion, an aberration leading to an abyss. Soon, however, one finds cheerful Elysium, the land of the blessed in ancient Greek mythology. From this place, through a flying buttress of the Eisenhart wall, one could once see the princely tomb on the Drehberg which was removed in 1828. An **orchard** in the same area, was restocked in 1992 with its original species and replanted in the original way. A **sandstone bench**, in the shape of an antique sarcophagus and decorated with reliefs depicting the fruit harvest, sits at the edge of the path.

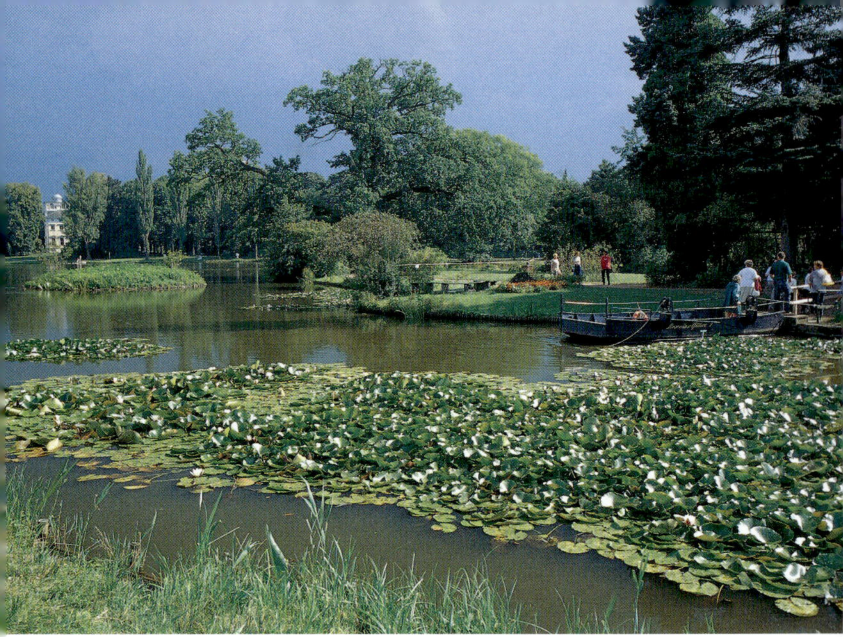

▲ *On Rose Island* [**18**]

Rousseau Island [**17**] located in front of Neumark Garden fits into the allegoric theme of the labyrinth as well. The 1782 monument, erected on the poplar lined island according to the design of Erdmannsdorff, bears an inscription on its pedestal which was written by the Prince himself. The monument represents the earliest replica of the tomb of Jean-Jacques Rousseau (1712–1778) in Ermenonville by Paris. Visitors coming from Dessau were here symbolically greeted in the "Garden of Enlightenment." **Rose Island** [**18**] located to the north of Neumark Garden, together with Swan Island positioned in front of it, exists, in its present-day form only since 1908, after soil filling and multiple reconfigurations. During the catastrophic flood of 1770/71, the original design of the **Island of the Princess** with a fishing hut was fragmented into four islands. Today's view is dominated by Prince Franz's planted oak tree, a pergola and ancient species of wild roses.

Schoch Garden

Schoch Garden, which represented the work place and residence of the most important gardeners of the Wörlitz grounds, was developed primarily between 1767 and 1790. It was named after its first gardener, Johann Leopold Ludwig Schoch (1728–1793). Located north of Wörlitz Lake, Schoch Garden is bordered by the Elbe's dyke, on the east by the Weidenheger and in the west by the Coswiger Chaussee. It is also divided into several garden areas. Located east of Wolf Canal, Schoch Island, with its arboretum around the Gothic House, Diana's Grove, and the garden areas at the Nymphaeum, took shape from 1767. The kitchen and flora gardens, the Romantic Enclave west of the Wolf Canal, and the grounds on the Elbe's dyke situated to the north, were developed in the 1780s. A beautiful view opens up from here onto the

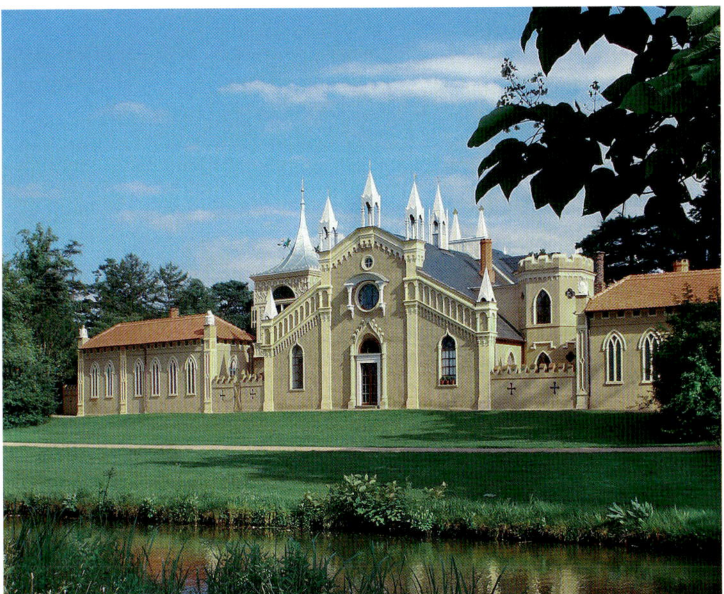

▲ *Gothic House* [20]

vast Elbe meadows. It is especially impressive to experience the water's force when the Elbe is flooding and water is reaching the Wörlitz dyke complex. Along a guided path, Schoch Garden reveals itself as a series of spatially-formed views, which change with every bend, evoking new impressions.

Built in 1811, **Wolf Bridge** [**19**] leads to Schoch Island over Wolf Canal. The sandstone bridge decorated with iron banister and cast iron vases was named after the farmer Wolf, who once cultivated his field here. The bridge is a striking spot in terms of the access view onto the garden one has from this location.

Passing through the subsequent arboretum, one reaches the **Gothic House** [**20**]. This example of very early neo-Gothic castle architecture was created according to the designs of Prince Franz, Erdmannsdorff, and Hesekiel. Initially, the Gothic House was built as a working and residential space for the gardeners. However, the Prince also used it for private stays and for housing various collections. He lived here for a longer period of time, together with the gardener's daughter Luise Schoch, who was later ennobled as Lady von Beringer. Until 1813, the house, inspired by the English Strawberry Hill (by Horace Walpole near London), was expanded again and again in several stages. During each construction phase, the architecture followed different models: the church Madonna dell'Orto in Venice on the canal side, English Tudor-Gothic Style on the garden side, the town hall in Wrocław (formerly Breslau) for the "New Tower." The neo-Gothic sandstone well standing in the southern courtyard, built in 1799, served as a water supply for the Gothic House and as refreshment for garden visitors. The Gothic House was surrounded by agricultural and orchard gardens. The Prince used the narrow elevated arboretum, surrounded by a belt-like path, for his experiments and studies in fruit cultivation and as a mulberry crop area for silkworm cultivation. In its initial stages, modern English farming techniques were exemplarily demonstrated on the agricultural fields nearby.

Within sight of the Gothic House, beyond the Large Meadow and below a grass hummock at the edge of the arboretum lies **Schoch's Crypt** [**21**]. This gravesite of the court's gardener (Johann Leopold

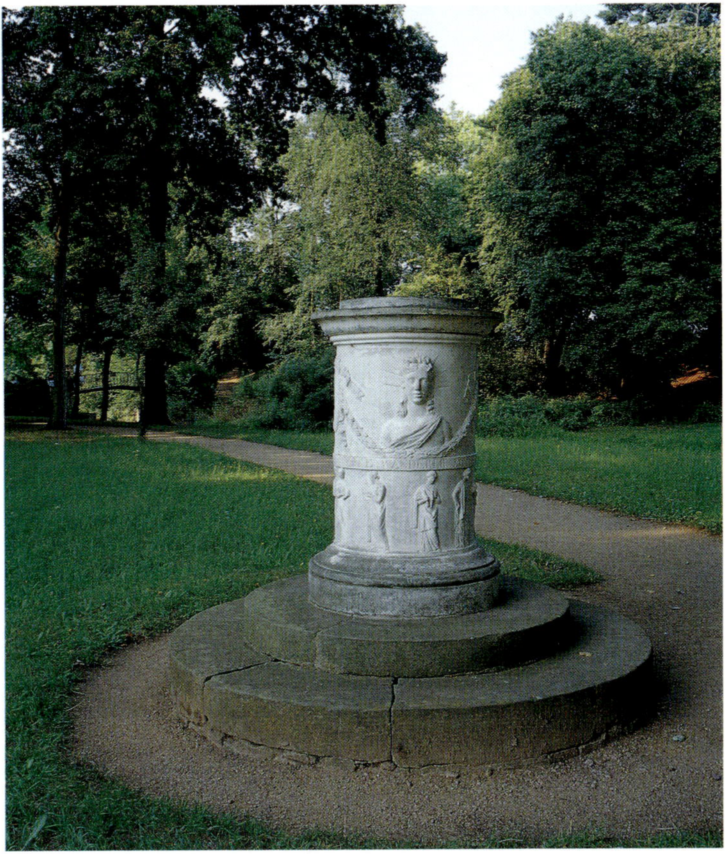

▲ *Warning Altar* [27]

Ludwig Schoch, Sr.) and his wife appreciatively recollects the Prince with an inscription.

In addition to Wolf Bridge, four other bridges lead to the island which was built up during the construction of the canal. **Hornzacken (Horn Spike) Bridge** [22], which was supposed to look like a split oak, was created in 1774 to connect the Gothic House with the agricultural garden beyond the canal. **White Bridge** [**23**] (also called Chinese or Stair Bridge) was inspired by William Chamber's palladium construction (a self-standing wooden arch construction) in Kew Gardens (London). It is found at the Small Walloch. Today, **Agnes Bridge** [**24**], built in 1958, stands in the same place where there once was a wooden swing bridge leading north towards the dyke. The sandstone **New Bridge** [**25**] enables passage to the Weidenheger. In 1810, it replaced an older wooden bridge from 1772. It is decorated with benches and relief representations of the goddess and god, Venus and Amor, surrounded by Tritons.

The **Small Walloch** (literarily, hole in the wall) is a body of water created by erosion. Around 1770, it was connected to the flow of water looping through Wolf Canal, Agnes Canal, and Suspension Bridge Canal. With **Diana's Grove** [**26**] on its eastern shore, it is consecrated to the goddess of the hunt. Close by a garden seat, one finds a two meter high **statue of Diana**, created around 1780 by the court sculptor Ehrlich.

The **Warning Altar** [**27**], 1.40 meters high and made of sandstone, stands east of the Agnes Bridge. It was created in spring of 1800 as a very early monument to art and nature conservation. Representations of Diana, Apollo, the nine muses, and the inscription, "Wanderer, pay heed to Nature and Art and their beautiful works." decorate the neoclassical altar.

The **Nymphaeum** [**28**], a garden seat designed by Erdmannsdorff in 1767/68 and dedicated to the water nymphs, is located on the southeastern grounds of Schoch Island. It was integrated into a former ice house. Around 1780, a wooden miner was placed in its access shaft. In the vault behind the Ionic columns, one finds the sculpture of a wrestler anointing himself (plaster cast). Goethe's inspiring words about his first visit to Wörlitz in 1778 are depicted on inscription tablets. In 1827, a vineyard was laid out on the eastern side of the hill next to the Nymphaeum.

Also belonging to Schoch Garden are the areas located west of Wolf Canal. Entering those grounds via the Hornzacken Bridge (Horn Spike

Temple of Flora [**32**] ▶

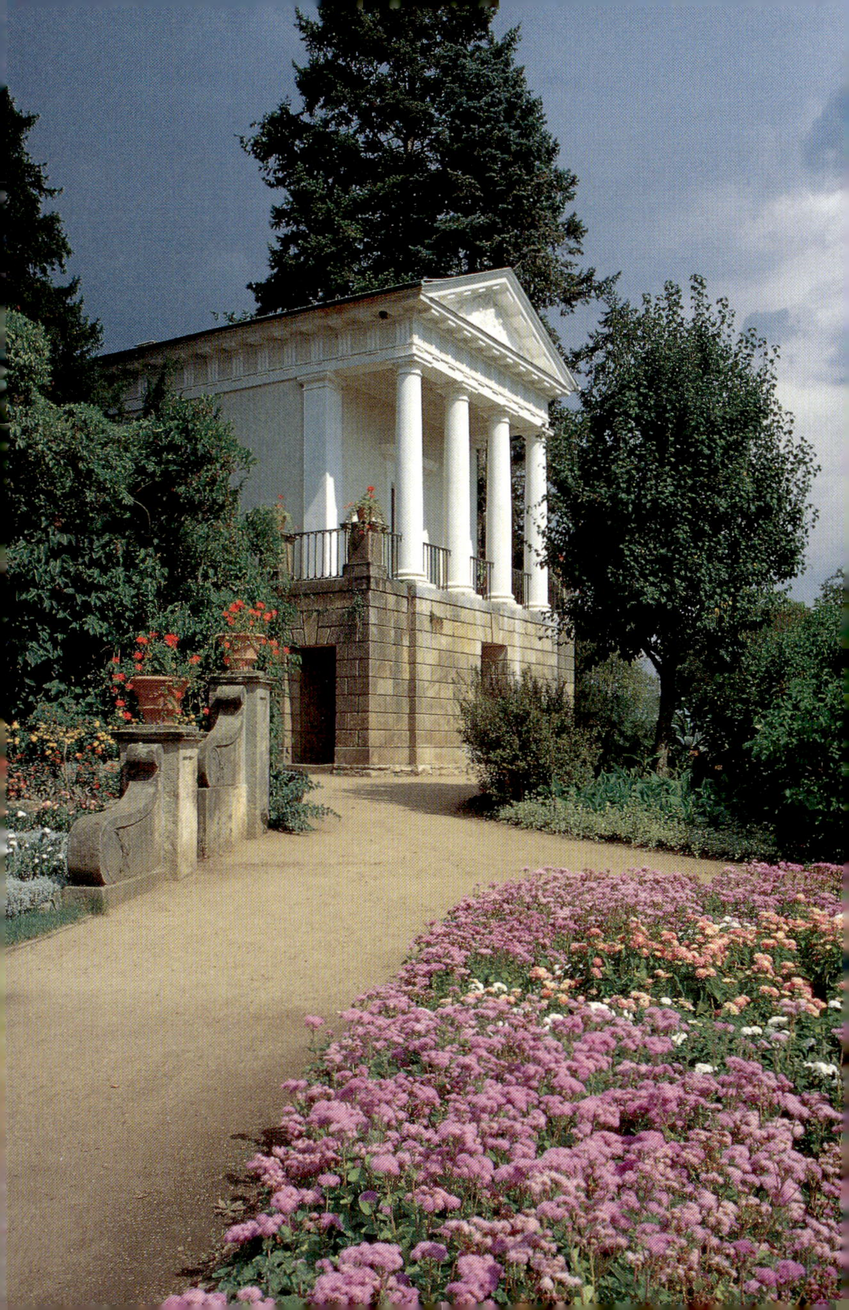

Bridge), one encounters the **cow barn** [29], which brings to mind the model farming once practiced here. The Neo-Gothic building listed around 1810 was used as a stable for English white cattle and sheep and subsequently converted into the gardener's residence. The adjoining grove of rhododendrons was created after 1900 at the same spot where the flower garden and English barns ("Kleediemen") belonging to the stable were once located. After 1790, the neo-classical **White Gate** [30], decorated with terracotta vases, was built into the wall of the kitchen's garden, which was planted with grapes and espalier fruit. The gate, created as a visual opening, reveals a picturesque view with the agricultural fields at the "New Path" as a scenic backdrop. From the start, **Flora's Garden** [31], dedicated to the goddess of flowers and youth, was decorated with flowers, which was unusual for an early landscaped garden. However, the **Palm Garden** (1895) and today's southern garden area (1923) were added later. A bronze imitation of Hermes taken from Herculaneum, also ended up in the garden, in 1914. The **Temple of Flora** [32], created by Erdmannsdorff according to a model of William Chamber's casino building in Wilton (South England), was used as a music pavilion and is decorated with an antique sculpture and floral wall paintings by the court painter Johann Fischer. The upper floor, used today for special collections, offers a view upon the phallus-shaped flower beds (dedicated to the fertility god, protector of fruit plants and gardens, Priapus) at the Gothic House. The **flower theatre**, outfitted with terracotta vases and sandstone troughs, in the form of an amphitheatre, was created as a location to display flower pots. West of Flora's Garden, there used to be an arboretum surround by a wall. Today, it is used by the cultural foundation as an agricultural area. After 1798/99, the neo-gothic **Palm House** (greenhouse) [33] replaced the winter gardens in the kitchen building and the Gothic House. In the 19th century, the **garden inspector residence** [34], built at the same time as the Palm House, became a depot for trading plants and seeds. The inspiration for this building was an English fishing house on the river Avon, which was depicted in Grohmann's *Magazine of Ideas* in 1796. The **forester's house** [35], located northwest of the court's garden nursery, was a square sandstone

Temple of Venus [38] ▶

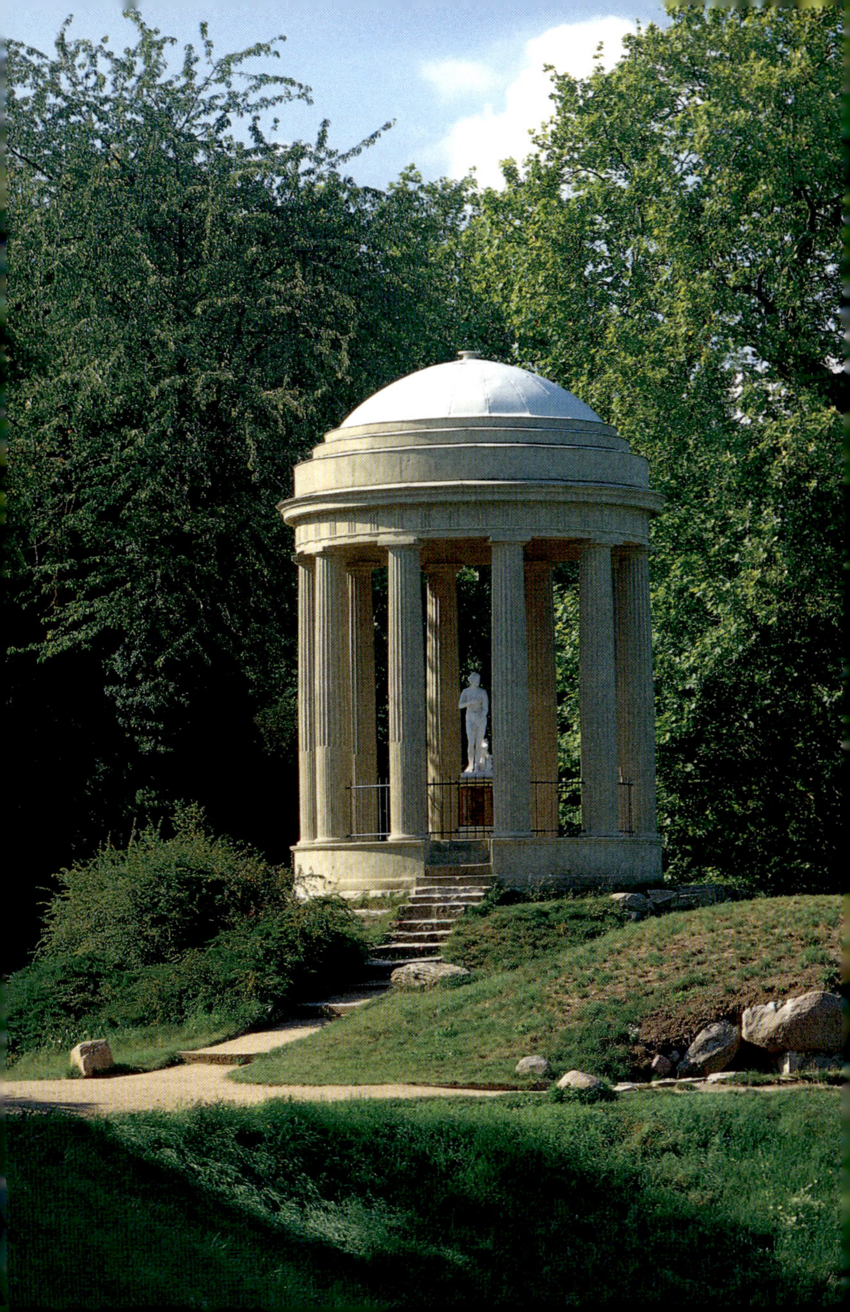

building with a tower set in front. Imitating the neo-gothic style of the court's nursery, it was only built in 1908.

In northern proximity to the dyke, the **Romantic Enclave** creates romanticized garden scenes using allegorical means of expression. One can reach the area by crossing the **Suspension Bridge** [**36**]. It consists of a wobbly hanging fixture spanning two artificial rock structures. Inspired by William Chambers (1726–1796), it was supposed to bewilder and frighten visitors. It was among the first attractions of the garden. Paths lead from a terrace next to the bridge to the residential and sleeping quarters, as well as to the hermit's retreat of prayer, and, further, the cell of the mystagogue. This carefully conceived garden program also incorporates ritual elements of freemasonry.

From **Luise Bluff** [**37**], (named after Princess Louise Charlotte of Sachsen-Gotha), a ruin-like rock formation with a neo-gothic oriel, created between 1794 and 1798, across the Elysian Valley, the path leads to the grottos located below the **Temple of Venus** [**38**]. The Doric sandstone rotunda built by Erdmannsdorff in 1794, with a copy of the Medici Venus, is an elevated focal point, from which one has a number of sight lines to landscape and garden features. The noble architecture was inspired by the Temple of Venus at Hadrian's Villa in Tivoli, as well as by its reconstructions in Stowe and Kew (England). The grottos located in the lower level are dedicated to the earth's elements, earth and fire, air, and water – and respectively to their gods – Vulcan, Aeolus, and Neptune. The grottoes are the final destination of the path of awareness which begins in the cell of the mystagogue. **Skald's Grave** [**39**], an earth mound surrounded by erratic boulders and located by the dyke further to the west, is dedicated to the Northern poets. Keeping east, also atop the dyke, one reaches the **Monument** [**40**], an irregular rock construction with an octagonal layout, which was built between 1801 and 1805. On its original observation deck, an antique Roman column made of granite is visible from afar. Prince Franz dedicated the building, located along the principle axis of the castle and outfitted with relief bust portraits of reigning Princes of Anhalt, to his ancestors.

Crocus meadow with the Monument [**40**] ▶

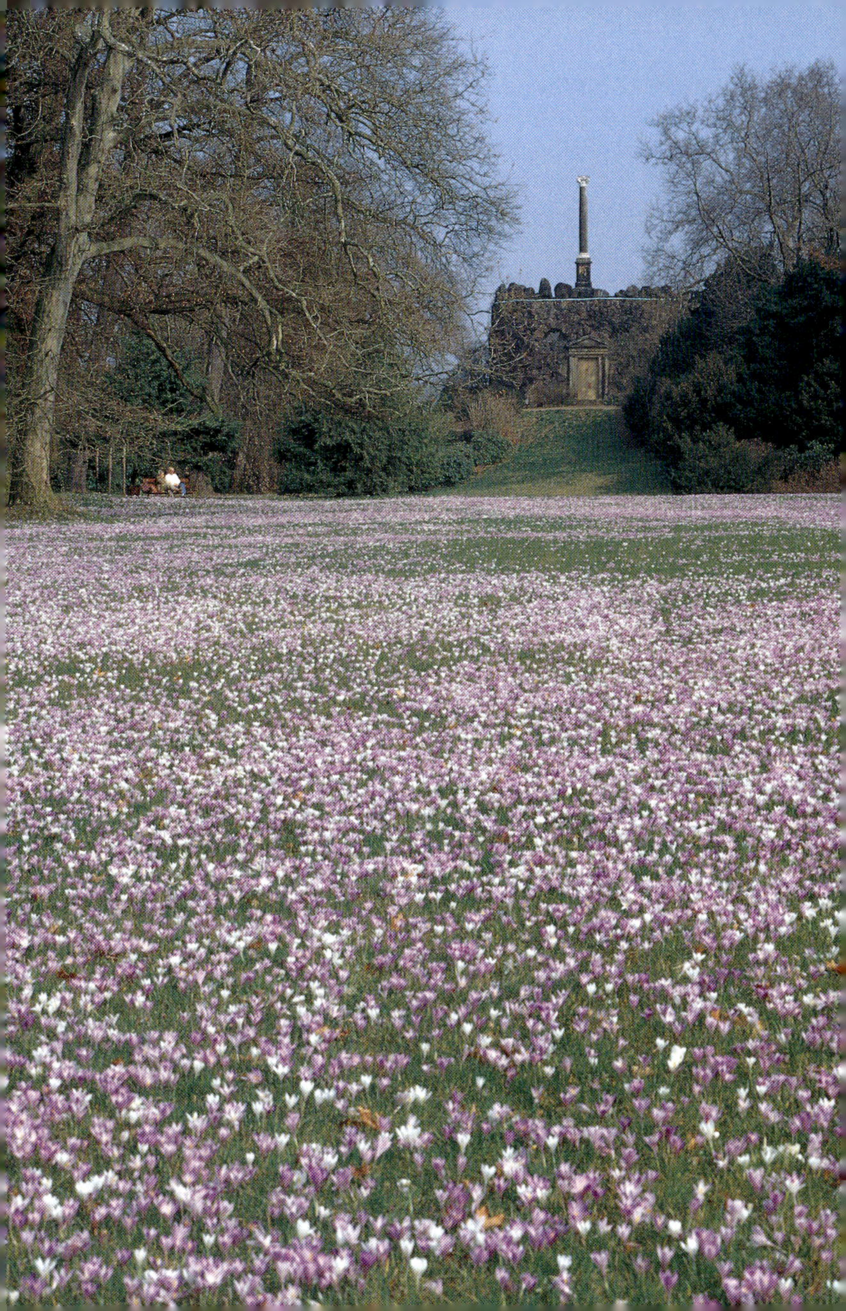

The Weidenheger

The garden on the Weidenheger, located between the Wörlitz Lake, Agnes Canal, and the Elbe's dyke, was created as part of the restoration efforts after the disastrous flood of 1770 and 1771. Until the completion of the New Grounds, it represented the eastern border of the Wörlitz arrangements. The additional areas, washed up by water, were protected and secured with willow and poplar plantings and the undestroyed inventory (the Golden Urn, and the Guardhouse "To the Horse") was preserved.

On the dyke above the **Golden Urn** [41], a place of repose has been formed from boulders as a look-out point, giving access to a panoramic view. The view in each direction is framed by two lime trees, and offers unique garden panoramas. Above the gold-plated sandstone tomb, designed by Erdmannsdorff in 1769 for the deceased eldest daughter of the ruling family, one can, from a grass hill lined by Lombardy poplars and red cedars at the edge of Agnes Canal, catch sight of the synagogue and the church side by side (front cover picture). The ensemble symbolizes the Prince's tolerant sensibility.

The **Guardhouse "To the Horse"** [42], a building designed by Erdmannsdorff with an Ionian sandstone temple façade and decorated with a bas-relief inspired by an antique tomb in Tivoli, was created in 1769, at the same time as the Golden Urn. East of here, as a terminus of several garden axes, (for example, as one comes from the shell nymph of the castle garden), one finds the **Thorn Extractor** (Spinario) [43], a larger-than-life sandstone replica of an antique sculpture, which was created by Johann Christian Pfeiffer in 1782. To reach the "Small Heger" and the **Venus Bath**, one crosses the Sun Canal via the **Swimming Bridge** (Ponton Bridge) [44] located further to the south. The small wooden bridge and the rose pergola found at this historic beach area are additions from the 19th century. The **Root Hut** (Bark House) [45] built in 1785, lined with bark, conifer cones, as well as straw, and outfitted with stone seats, served as a bath house. Leading through this house, the path continues to a larger-than-life sandstone sculpture, the **Kneeling Venus** [46], which was crafted by Pfeiffer in

Thorn Extractor [43] ▶

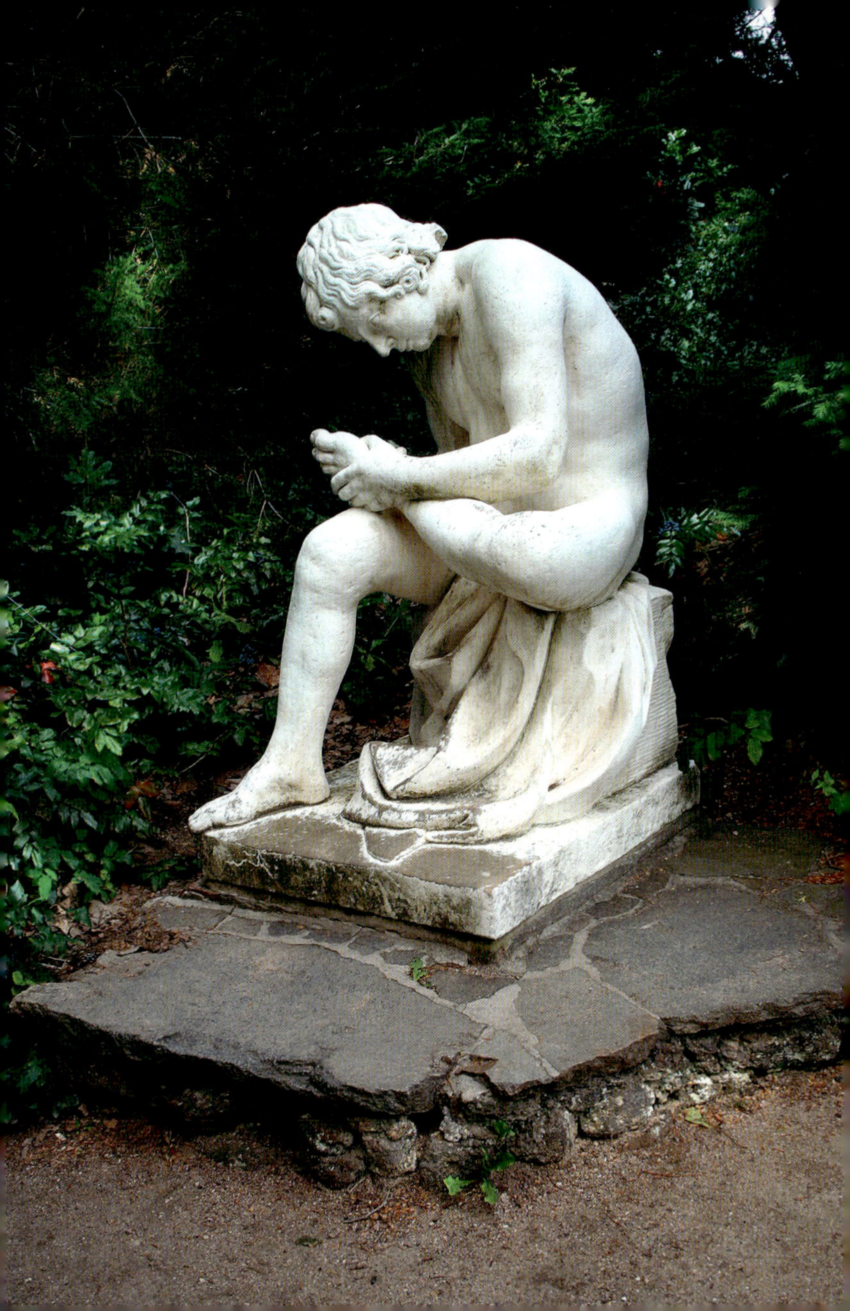

1782 at the northernmost official ferry landing and modelled after an antique work in the Villa Medici (Rome).

New Grounds

The layout of the New Grounds, visually focused on the Great Walloch and Rock ("Stein") Island, was largely created by the gardener's son, Johann George Schoch, Jr. (1758–1826). The New Grounds represent the last large extension of the garden. The wide-ranging landscape of this area of the garden is bounded by Wörlitz Lake in the south, the Elbe's dyke in the north, the Wassermühlenfahrt (Water Mill Drive) in the east, and the Weidenheger in the west. A few garden buildings in the style of "travel impressions" as well as gallery plantings, dominate the large agricultural and wet areas.

The artificial **Rock "Stein" Island,** [**47**], was created between 1788 and 1794 in the southeast of the Wörlitz garden realm. Various citations of Italy, including the Gulf of Naples, details from a gladiator school in Taormina, a columbarium, Roman baths, grottos, an amphitheatre and the Villa Hamilton, are evoked in miniature form on this strange multi-level structure surrounded by large boulders. A replica of Mount Vesuvius towers over everything and was illuminated for special events in its early years. The adjacent ruin of **Egeria's Grotto** [**48**], created in 1790 and modelled after a Roman example, with a larger-than-life sandstone sculpture of Egeria, Nymph of the Spring, surrounds the place alleged to be the source of the Wörlitz bodies of water.

Wandering through the "Italian landscape" north of "Stein" along George Canal, one reaches the **Iron Bridge** [**49**]. Located in proximity to a ford, the bridge is a 1791 miniature reproduction (scale 1:4) of Wilkinson's – at the time – state-of-the-art cast iron bridge in Coalbrookdale (Shropshire). It is situated at the entrance of George Valley, a garden landscape enhanced with stone seats, which Prince Franz named after his brother Johann Georg. The originally gold-plated **Sun Bridge** [**50**] was erected in 1796. Its radial iron decoration positioned at the bridge's arch, together with its reflection in the water, was supposed to appear like the corona of the sun and refer to Inka culture.

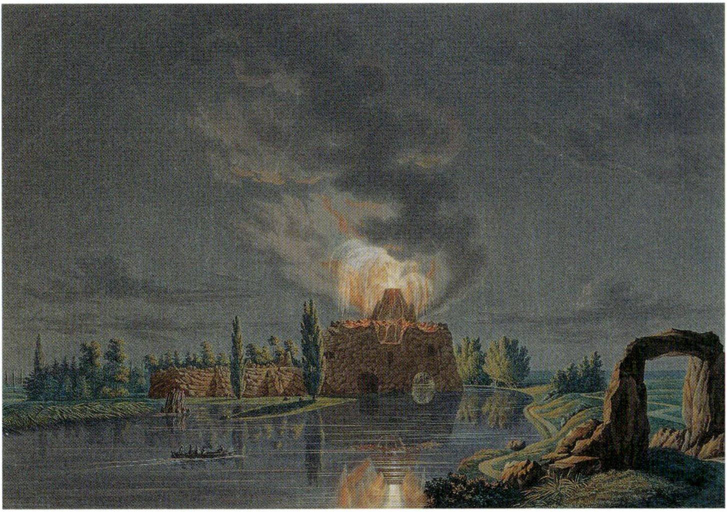

▲ *Rock "Stein" Island, aquatint by Karl Kurtz*

It leads to the artistically modelled landscape at the **Great Walloch** (also referred to as "Bürgerkolk" – "Citizen's Crater"), a body of water with two islands which was laid out in the last decade of the 18th century. Here, on top of the Elbe's dyke, arises the **Pantheon** [**51**] built by Erdmannsdorff between 1795 and 1797. It houses the collection of classical antiquities acquired in 1796. According to an inscription at the entrance, the three story rotunda with a portico of four columns, topped by a triangular pediment, including a viewing platform, is dedicated to "the friends of Nature and of Art." Outfitted with replicas of Egyptian art, the ground level is enclosed by the broadened dyke.

Amalie Grotto [**52**] on Amalie Island, originally a headland in the Large Walloch, was built by Hesekiel in 1793. The island was considered a popular destination for gondola tours and garden festivities. It is named after the designated heir Princess Christiane Amalie (1774–1846). The crowning vine arbour is decorated with sandstone herms of

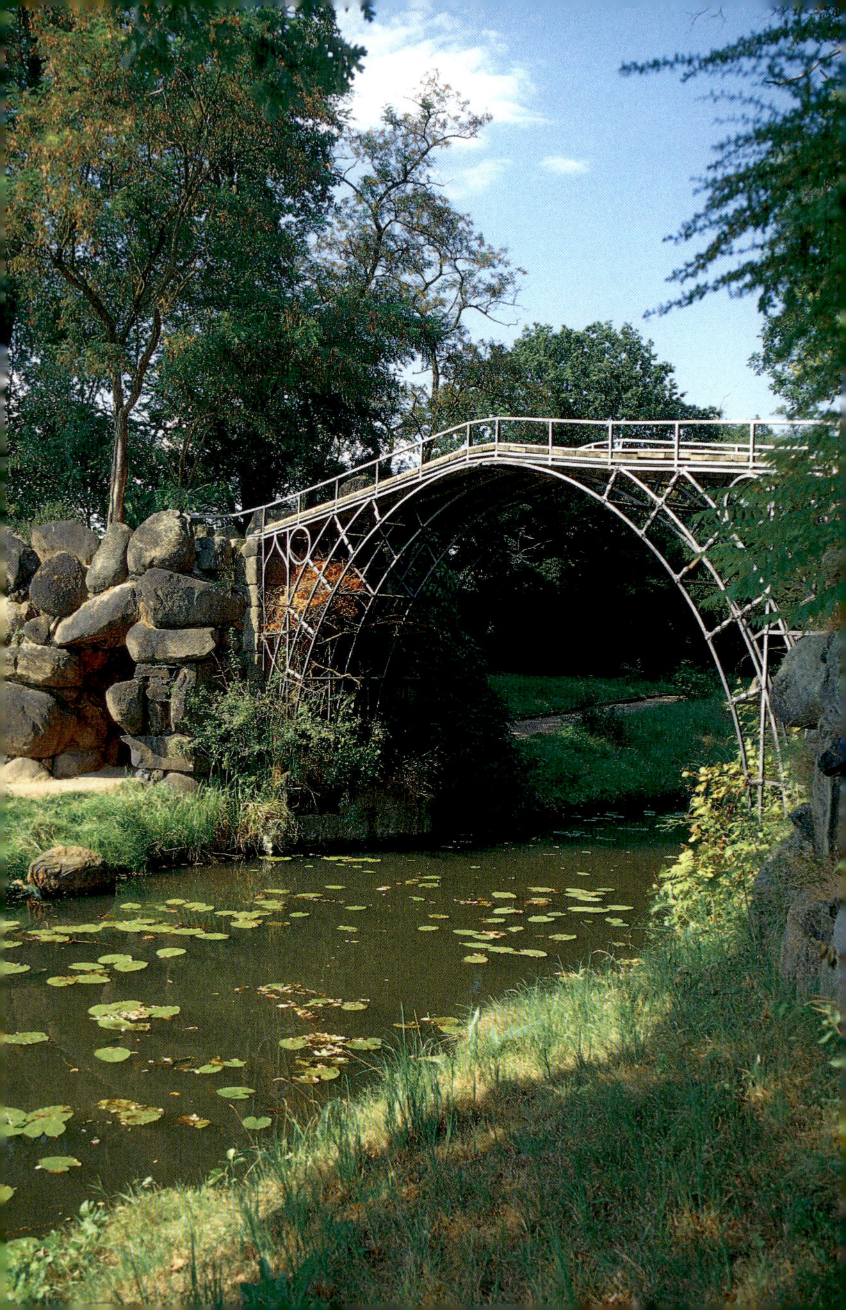

the ancient Greek lyric poets Sappho and Anacreon, whose gazes are directed at the adjoining **Island of the Commemoration of the Dead**. At this "destination of water excursions," one can find stone seats for moments of rest and a sandstone monument (cippus) which was erected in 1797 and bears inscriptions from texts by Johann Gottfried Herder: "We are all mortals and mortal are all our aspirations; suffering and joy, they pass, or we pass them." The **Red Dyke Guardhouse** [**53**], occasionally occupied by the Prince, was developed from a design by Erdmannsdorff in 1772. It stands in visual relationship to the Proteus Stone on the east shore of the Large Walloch. A small **bridge made out of a split oak trunk** [**54**] leads from here across the historical tributary water of the Wörlitz Lake to the **Piedmont Farmhouse** [**55**], constructed in 1792/93 by Hesekiel. According to legend, this plastered brick architecture standing on cliffs was donated and inspired by Grand Duke Carl August von Sachsen-Weimar-Eisenach (1757–1828), who visited Wörlitz together with Goethe on a regular basis.

A Garden without a Fence: A Look at the Other Side

Today, the Wörlitz garden grounds are overseen and maintained by the cultural foundation of Dessau-Wörlitz. The area of 276.8 acres (112 hectares) was a result of the breakup of land into different trusts following the expropriation of the princes in the 1920s. The holistic art experience (Gesamtkunstwerk) was originally much more extensive and commenced from afar, as soon as Wörlitz came into view. Münsterberg, Drehberg, Berting, and Riesigk could be seen as the actual entryways to the Wörlitz grounds. The city itself stands in a uniquely deliberate relationship to the garden grounds. Striking and symbolically-rich architectural sites visually connect with various elements of the park. Similarly, a rich storehouse of ideas and historical associations continually offers opportunities of connecting to the overall program of the park.

The lay-out of the entrance to the city from the park was designed by Erdmannsdorff as allegories of life carried over into life: The **Old School in Griesen** from 1788 highlights efforts of educating the country's citizens, the **Domaine** (communal farm) [**56**], built between 1783 and 1787 and modelled after Palladio's Villa Emo, documents exem-

◀ *Iron Bridge* [**49**]

plary, up-to-date agricultural methods. In 1790, the **Jewish Cemetery** was developed at the southern entrance to the city; in the southern quarter of the city lies the **Christian Cemetery** [**57**] with the custodian's house built in 1795. At the southern end of the market place – modelled freely after ancient arenas during the founding era – stands the pavilion-like **city hall** [**58**], which was erected between 1792 and 1795 in Palladian style. This civic ensemble corresponds with the entrance to the garden and the castle; the city assembly and the princely residence seem here to stand in symbolic dialogue with each other, underlining again the liberal and enlightened sentiments, which were carried into life in a unique way at Wörlitz.

Quoted Literature and Further Reading

Alex, R., *Wörlitz*. Leipzig, 1991. – Boettiger, C. A., *Reise nach Wörlitz 1797*. Edited from the original manuscript and with explanatory notes by E. Hirsch. Wörlitz, 1999 (8). – Grohmann, J. G., *Ideenmagazin für Liebhaber von Gärten*, Issue no. 1. Leipzig, 1796. – Harksen, M.-L., *Stadt, Schloß und Park Wörlitz. Die Kunstdenkmale des Landes Anhalt*, vol. 2.2. Burg, 1939. Reprint Halle, 1998. – Hirsch, E., *Dessau-Wörlitz. Aufklärung und Frühklassik*. Leipzig/München, 1985. – Matthisson, F. von, *Erinnerungen*, 2nd book. Zürich, 1825. – Rode, A., Ross, H. and Trauzettel, L., *Der Englische Garten zu Wörlitz*. Berlin, 1994 (2). – Rode, A., *Beschreibung des Fürstlichen Anhalt-Dessauischen Landhauses und Englischen Gartens zu Wörlitz*. Dessau, 1798 (2). – Trauzettel, L., "Das Gartenreich von Dessau-Wörlitz." In *Gärten der Goethezeit*, pp. 45–75, edited by H. Günther. Leipzig, 1993. – Trauzettel, L., Wörlitz, *Führer durch die Englischen Anlagen*. München (2), 1991. – Trauzettel, L., "Wanderer, achte Natur und Kunst und schone ihrer Werke. Ideengehalt und Wiederherstellung der Wörlitzer Anlagen." In *Garten – Kunst – Denkmalpflege, Festschrift D. Hennebo*. Worms, 1994.– Trauzettel, L., "Gartenkünstler und Gartenkunst in Wörlitz." In *Weltbild Wörlitz: Entwurf einer Kulturlandschaft*. Wörlitz, 1996. – Trauzettel, L., "Beiträge über Oranienbaum,Wörlitz, Großkühnau und das Gartenreich." In *Unendlich schön – Das Dessau Wörlitzer Gartenreich*. Berlin, 2005.

Amalie Grotto [**52**] *at the Great Walloch* ▶